GN00722470

Beverly Clark's
Wedding Toasts

BEVERLY CLARK'S

Wedding
Toasts

RUNNING PRESS

PHILADELPHIA • LONDON

Library of Congress Cataloging-in-Publication
Number 99-74348

ISBN 0-7624-0736-0

This book may be ordered by mail from the publisher.
Please include $1.00 for postage and handling.
But try your bookstore first!

Running Press Book Publishers
125 South Twenty-second Street
Philadelphia, Pennsylvania 19103-4399

Visit us on the web!
www.runningpress.com

Contents

Wedding feasts mean wedding toasts—the more, the merrier. The custom of drinking a toast to the happiness and good fortune of the bride and groom has become an essential ingredient of any wedding celebration. It allows the participants to express the collective joy and love felt by everyone in attendance. For many, however, the task of finding the right words to express these sentiments is a challenging one.

The bachelor party, the rehearsal dinner, and the reception are perfect occasions for guests and participants alike to raise their glasses to the bride and groom. Similarly, these events are wonderful opportunities for the bride

and groom to thank their friends and family for the help and support they have provided throughout the years. Toasts need not be literary masterpieces. If you speak from the heart, you will reach your audience and move them as well.

Within these pages, renowned wedding consultant Beverly Clark gathers traditions, tips, guidelines, and classic quotations to aid any aspiring speaker in the daunting quest to prepare the perfect toast. You'll find everything you need to create toasts from the heart, that are infused with wisdom, humor, and love.

Toasting
Etiquette

Toasting dates back to ancient times. Originally, "toast" referred to a piece of burnt, spiced bread, which was dropped into a glass of wine to improve the flavor of the drink and to help absorb the sediment. The term soon came to refer to the drink itself.

When toasting first began, it was common practice for men to hold daggers or other weapons in their right hand or to conceal them in their clothing. The traditional toast giver's position—glass held high in the right hand, arm extended straight from the shoulder—proved the toast giver's peaceful intentions by showing that he neither held nor concealed a weapon.

Some time after the seventeenth century, it became common to clink glasses after the toast was given, and before it was drunk. This tradition may be linked to a belief that all five senses should be involved in the act of drinking. With the clink, the drink is smelled, tasted, seen, touched, and finally, heard. It may also be linked to early belief in the power of noise to frighten away evil spirits.

Asian countries have strong traditions of toasting. In Korea, the glass is emptied and the last few drops are shaken out. A glass is never refilled until it is completely empty. In Japan, however, the glass is constantly refilled so it is never empty.

To your good health, old friend,
may you live for a thousand years,
and I be there to count them.

Robert Smith Surtees (1803–1864)
English writer

Traditionally, the festivities at the bachelor party begin with a dinner where the groom makes a Champagne toast to his bride. In days past, each man would smash his glass after the toast, ensuring that it could never be used for a less worthy purpose. The tradition is rarely carried to this extreme anymore, but the chivalrous groom will still toast his bride.

The bridesmaids' party has become another popular occasion for toasting. Etiquette states that here, the bride proposes a toast to the groom.

Toasts are a fun and important part of personalizing your rehearsal dinner. This is usually a more casual event that includes those individuals closest to the bride and groom—a perfect occasion for guests to tell personal anecdotes about the couple.

Traditionally, the hosts of the dinner, usually the groom's parents, begin the toasting by welcoming the guests. They may choose to toast the couple at this point or later in the evening. The best man is the other typical toast giver at this specific occasion. The groom's family may also open up the toasts to the guests.

The bride and groom traditionally toast their families, their
attendants, and each other at the
close of the rehearsal dinner. If
they haven't already done so, the
couple may present their attendants with their gifts at this time.

Traditionally, the honor of the first toast at the reception is given to the best man. He commands the guests' attention at any time after the receiving line, and after the guests have been served a toasting beverage. He should begin by referring to his relationship with the couple and then proceed to wish them a long and happy life together.

The traditional beverage for toasting is Champagne; however, white wine or punch is often served. Once the toast is proposed, the guests stand (if seated), hold up their glasses, and then drink to the couple. The bride and groom do not stand or drink when they are being toasted.

Champagne, inseparable companion
of joyous heavenly events, crown
of festivities and special celebrations.
Champagne, symbol of friendship,
toast of state banquets, torch that kin-
dles the light of triumph, ritual that
launches steamships and airplanes!
Remembrance of rebirth, joyful tear
of anniversary, stamp of victory and
peace, holy dedication of love.

Geneviève Dévignes
French historian

A case of Champagne containing twelve bottles will serve seventy-five guests. You will need to provide— at minimum—enough Champagne to fill each guest's glass once. The price of Champagne varies widely, so set a budget and choose the best Champagne that you can afford.

Come quickly, I am tasting stars!

Dom Pérignon (1638–1715)
French Benedictine monk

Although the groom traditionally follows the best man at the reception, many brides and grooms choose to have the maid or matron of honor speak next. In this case, the groom, who graciously toasts his bride, his parents, and his new in-laws, follows her. Then comes the bride, followed by the groom's parents.

Other guests or members of the bridal party may want to propose a toast as well. It is best if the toasting is limited to a few. Once the toasting is over the best man reads any congratulatory telegrams, and the newlyweds share the first dance.

Finding the
Perfect Words

The honor of giving a toast at a wedding can seem burdensome and frightening at first. After all, you've been asked to speak in front of numerous people, many of whom you may know only slightly or not at all. Remain calm and try to keep things in perspective. Your friends and family are a forgiving audience. They do not expect perfection—kind words, thoughtfully spoken, will satisfy. Use the following tips to create a personal speech that speaks to your relationship with those being honored.

For thousands of years the purpose of toasts has remained twofold: to honor loved ones and to wish them good health and happiness. Your speech should follow these time-tested guidelines. Here is a chance to share something meaningful about the people you care about. Remember that this is their moment, not yours.

Try to write your toast well in advance of the event. You may be tempted to "wing it," but this is generally not a good idea. If you take time to prepare, you'll be far more comfortable and far less likely to say something inappropriate.

Practice your toast as often
as you can. Read it aloud and
memorize it if at all possible.
The more familiar you are with
what it is you want to say, the
more relaxed you'll be when it
comes time to say it.

Practice is the best
of all instructors.

Publilius Syrus
(1st century B.C.)
Roman writer

he first and most impor-
tant rule is to be brief.
Your speech should only
last two to four minutes. If you
drone on for longer than five
minutes, you risk losing much of
your audience and lessening the
impact of your words.

Brevity is the soul of wit.

William Shakespeare (1564–1616)
English writer

Take your toast seriously, but try to incorporate at least one funny story or anecdote. The best formula is to start out with a humorous moment and then build to a more sentimental conclusion. You want your speech to be heartfelt, but not overly emotional. Weddings are joyous events and your toast should be joyous as well.

Avoid vulgar or embarrassing
stories and jokes. Remember that
your audience is composed of
grandparents, parents, and others
who might be offended by your
words. Always err on the side of
caution—if you question whether
a specific item is appropriate,
steer clear.

Keep your alcohol consumption to a minimum before giving your toast. While many toast givers drink a beer or two to bolster their courage and calm their jitters, inebriated toasters are far more likely to embarrass others and themselves. Many couples choose to videotape the toasts at their reception, and you do not want your slurred words haunting you for years to come.

Where the drink goes in,
there the wit goes out.

George Herbert (1593–1633)
English poet

Speak slowly, distinctly, and loudly. Many toasts are mumbled, leaving guests in the back of the reception hall wondering what you've said. You don't want anyone to miss your words.

You should end your toast with a formal salute to the honoree or honorees. For example: "A toast to John and Jane and their eternal happiness!" This tells the guests that your toast has ended and lets them know what to say as they raise their glasses.

Traditional
Toasts

May your neighbors respect you,

Trouble neglect you,

The angels protect you,

And heaven accept you.

May the Irish hills caress you.

May her lakes and rivers bless you.

May the luck of the Irish
    enfold you.

May the blessings of
    Saint Patrick behold you.

—Irish toast

Here's to the bride
and the bridegroom,

We'll ask their success
in our prayers,

And through life's dark
shadows and sunshine

That good luck may
always be theirs.

—Armenian toast

May your eyes
stay filled
with stars and
your hearts with visions
of dreams yet to come.

—traditional wedding toast

Lucky stars above you,

Sunshine on your way,

Many friends to love you,

Joy in work and play,

Laughter to outweigh each care,

In your heart a song.

And gladness waiting everywhere

All your whole life long!

—traditional Irish toast

He who doesn't risk never
gets to drink Champagne.

—Russian proverb

Now you will feel no rain, for each
of you will be shelter to the other.
Now you will feel no cold, for each
of you will be warmth to the other.
Now there is no more loneliness.
Now there are two persons, but one
life before you. Go now to your
dwelling, to enter in to the days of
your life together. And may your days
be good and long upon the Earth.

—from an Apache Indian
wedding ceremony

Here's to marriage, that happy estate that resembles a pair of scissors—so joined that they cannot be separated, often moving in opposite directions, yet punishing anyone who comes between them.

Sydney Smith (1771–1845)
English clergyman and writer

May you have all
the happiness

And luck that life
can hold—

And at the end of
all your rainbows,

May you find a pot
of gold.

—traditional Irish toast

Here's to us that are here,
to you that are there, and
the rest of us everywhere.

Rudyard Kipling (1865–1936)
English writer

May you grow old on one pillow.

—Armenian toast

Were't the last drop in the well,

An I gasp'd upon the brink,

Ere my fainting spirit fell,

'Tis to thee that I would drink.

George Gordon,
Lord Byron (1788–1824)
English poet

Heaven give you many,

many, merry days!

William Shakespeare (1564–1616)
English poet and playwright

Drink to me only with thine eyes,

And I will pledge with mine;

Or leave a kiss within the cup,

And I'll not look for wine.

Ben Jonson (1572–1637)
English writer

Here's to the freedom and
pleasures of single life. . . .
May my memory now fail me.

Michael Macfarlane
American writer

When the first light of sun—
   Bless you.

When the long day is done—
   Bless you.

In your smiles and your tears—
   Bless you.

Through each day of your years—
   Bless you.

—traditional Irish blessing

On Friendship
and Family

A friend is one who
dislikes the same people
you dislike.

Anonymous

Each friend represents a world in us, a world possibly not born until they arrive, and it is only by this meeting that a new world is born.

Anaïs Nin (1903–1977)
French writer

I want someone to laugh with me, someone to be grave with me, someone to please me and help my discrimination with his or her own remark, and at times, no doubt, to admire my acuteness and penetration.

Robert Burns (1759–1796)
Scottish poet

My true friends have always
given me that supreme proof
of devotion, a spontaneous
aversion for the man I loved.

Colette, Sidonie-Gabrielle
(1873–1954)
French writer

rief can take care
of itself, but to
get the full value
of joy you must have some-
body to divide it with.

Mark Twain (1835–1910)
American writer

The best friend is likely to
acquire the best wife, because
a good marriage is based on
the talent for friendship.

Friedrich Nietzsche (1844–1900)
German philosopher

Family is one of
nature's masterpieces.

George Santayana (1863–1952)
Spanish writer

Home is having a large, loving, caring, close-knit family in another city.

George Burns (1896–1996)
American comedian

My father has given me the greatest treasure a father can give—a piece of himself.

Suzanne Chazin
American writer

Fathers are what give daughters away to other men who aren't nearly good enough, so they can have grandchildren who are smarter than anybody's.

Paul Harvey
American broadcaster

There are only two lasting
bequests we can hope to give
our children. One of these is
roots, the other, wings.

Hodding Carter (1907–1972)
American writer

In love to our wives there is desire,
to our sons there is ambition;
but in that to our daughters there
is something which there are no
words to express.

Joseph Addison (1672–1719)
English writer

When I was a boy of fourteen, my father was so ignorant I could hardly stand to have the old man around. But when I got to be twenty-one, I was astonished at how much he had learned in seven years.

Mark Twain (1835–1910)
American writer

No man can possibly know what life means, what the world means, what anything means, until he has a child and loves it. And then the whole universe changes and nothing will ever again seem exactly as it seemed before.

Lafcadio Hearn (1850–1904)
Greek-American writer

Are there any brothers who
do not criticize a bit and
make fun of the fiancé who is
stealing a sister from them?

Colette, Sidonie-Gabrielle
(1873–1954)
French writer

The love of a good mother for her children is in a class by itself. In other words, it is unique, especially unique in fact. Unique because there is nothing like it in this big world. . . . Especially unique because it is ever-trustful, ever-devoted, ever-forgiving, ever-tender, ever-unchanging, and ever-enduring.

Samuel Johnson (1709–1784)
English writer

Fifty-four years of love and tender-
ness and crossness and devotion and
unswerving loyalty. Without (my
mother) I could not have achieved a
quarter of what I have achieved, not
only in terms of success and career,
but in terms of personal happiness. . . .
She has never stood between me and
my life, never tried to hold me too
tightly, always let me go free. . . .

Noël Coward (1899–1973)
English playwright and actor

All that I am or hope to be,

I owe to my angel mother.

Abraham Lincoln (1809–1865)
American President

A mother is not a person to
lean on but a person to make
leaning unnecessary.

Dorothy Canfield Fisher (1879–1958)
American writer

God could not be everywhere,
and therefore he made mothers.

—Jewish proverb

On Love and
Marriage

Love is patient and kind. Love envies
no one, is never boastful, never
conceited, never rude; love is never
selfish, never quick to take offense.
Love keeps no score of wrongs, takes
no pleasure in the sins of others, but
delights in the truth. There is nothing
love cannot face; there is no limit to
its faith, its hope, its endurance.

The Bible, 1 Corinthians 13:4–7

Two such as you with
   such a master speed

Cannot be parted nor be
   swept away

From one another once you
   are agreed

That life is only life
   forevermore

Together wing to wing and
   oar to oar.

Robert Frost (1874–1963)
American poet

Grow old with me!

The best is yet to be,

The last of life,

For which, the first is made.

Robert Browning (1812–1889)
English poet

Happiness resides not in possessions and not in gold; the feeling of happiness dwells in the soul.

Democritus (460–370 B.C.)
Greek philosopher

The man or woman you really
love will never grow old to
you. Through the wrinkles of
time, through the bowed frame
of years, you will always see
the dear face and feel the warm
heart union of your eternal love.

Alfred A. Montapert
American writer

What is love? Love is something that makes two people think they are pretty even when nobody else does. It also makes them sit close together on a bench even when there's plenty of room. It's something which makes two people very quiet when you are around. . . . And that's all I know about love until I grow up.

(Written by a ten year old named
Tommy for his school composition.)
Charlie W. Shedd
American writer

I learned the real meaning of love. Love is absolute loyalty. People fade, looks fade, but loyalty never fades. You can depend so much on certain people, you can set your watch by them. And that's love, even if it doesn't seem very exciting.

Sylvester Stallone
American actor

Love is an act of endless
forgiveness.

Peter Ustinov
English actor

There is only one termi-
nal dignity—love. And
the story of a love is not
important—what is important is
that one is capable of love. It is
perhaps the only glimpse we are
permitted of eternity.

Helen Hayes (1900–1993)
American actor

Come live with me,
    and be my love,

And we will some
    new pleasures prove

Of golden sands,
    and crystal brooks,

With silken lines,
    and silver hooks.

John Donne (1572–1631)
English poet

What greater thing is there
for two human souls than to
feel that they are joined . . . to
strengthen each other . . . (and)
to be one with each other in
silent unspeakable memories.

George Eliot (1819–1880)
English writer

The unit of the wife and husband begins as a fresh creation, as innocent and full of promise as any newborn.

Arlene Hamilton Stewart
American writer

That which we love,

we come to resemble.

St. Bernard of Clairvaux (1090–1153)
French religious saint

Marriage is not just communion and passionate embraces; marriage is also three meals a day, sharing the workload, and remembering to take out the trash.

Joyce Brothers
American psychologist

Marriage is a partnership in which each inspires the other, and brings fruition to both of you.

Millicent Carey McIntosh
American writer

A successful marriage is an edifice
that must be rebuilt every day.

André Maurois (1885–1967)
French historian and writer

S uccess in marriage
does not come merely
through finding
the right mate, but through
being the right mate.

Barnett Brickner
American rabbi

Weddings are for optimists.
We enter into them with
the greatest goodwill we can
bear for another person.

Arlene Hamilton Stewart
American writer

Marriage is happiness,

success, purity.

Melvin Wilkerson
American law
enforcement officer

Love doesn't just sit there, like a
stone; it has to be made, like bread,
remade all the time, made new.

Ursula Le Guin
American writer

The day-to-day companionship—
the pleasure in doing things together,
or in doing separate things but in
delighting to exchange experiences—
is a continuous and central part of
what a man and woman who love
each other can share.

Susan Okin
American writer

There are as many kinds of love
as many kinds of light,

And every kind of love makes
a glory in the night.

There is love that stirs the heart,
and love that gives it rest,

But the love that leads life upwards
is the noblest and the best.

Henry Van Dyke (1852–1933)
American writer and clergyman

For one human being to love another: that is perhaps the most difficult of all our tasks, the ultimate, the last test and proof, the work for which all other work is but preparation.

Rainer Maria Rilke (1875–1926)
German poet

There are in the end three things
that last: faith, hope, and love,
and the greatest of these is love.

The Bible, 1 Corinthians 13:13

This book has been bound using
handcraft methods, and is
Smyth-sewn to ensure durability.

The dust jacket and interior were
designed by Frances J. Soo Ping Chow.

The text was compiled by
Elaine M. Bucher.

The text was edited by Caroline Tiger.

The text was set in
Palace Script and Weiss.